AF131345

BOOK ANALYSIS

By Benjamin Taylor

Keep the Aspidistra Flying

by George Orwell

Bright
≡Summaries.com

GEORGE ORWELL

ENGLISH NOVELIST AND JOURNALIST

- **Born in Motihari (India) in 1903.**
- **Died in London in 1950.**
- **Notable works:**
  - *Homage to Catalonia* (1938), autobiographical account
  - *Animal Farm* (1945), novel
  - *1984* (1949), novel

George Orwell is the pen name of Eric Blair, one of the best-known and most highly regarded writers of the 20th century, whose novels and essays are quoted around the world. He was born into an upper-middle-class, but not rich, family and won a scholarship to Eton in 1917. On leaving school, he joined the imperial police in Burma and remained there until 1927, when he grew tired of upholding the oppressive colonial regime. On returning to England, he set about writing a series of fiction and non-fiction novels and pieces of journalism, many of which feature social criticism and support for Democratic Socialism. In 1936 he journeyed to Spain to fight against Franco's Fascist forces in the Spanish Civil War. He was wounded and recorded his time in Spain and the political atmosphere there in Homage to Catalonia. During the Second World War, he worked for the BBC and began writing Animal Farm, an allegorical novel exploring the distortions of the Russian Revolution. He finished his final novel, 1984, shortly before his death from tuberculosis in 1950. Though a highly elusive and almost mythic figure in English literary history, Orwell has left a legacy of highlighting social injustice and fighting against oppression that has inspired millions around the world.

KEEP THE ASPIDISTRA FLYING

MONEY MATTERS

- **Genre:** novel
- **Reference edition:** Orwell, G. (1998) *Keep the Aspidistra Flying*. London: Martin Secker & Warburg Limited.
- **1st edition:** 1936
- **Themes:** money, class, London, British society, work, family, poverty, Capitalism

Keep the Aspidistra Flying was written during 1934 and 1935 and draws upon Orwell's time working in a bookshop in Hampstead, London, as well as his time tramping round London (as described in his 1933 social documentary work *Down and Out in Paris and London*). The novel was published in 1936 by Orwell's long-time publisher Victor Gollancz to largely positive reviews. In particular, it was widely praised for the accuracy of its depiction of the alienation and loneliness of poverty, as well as the poor conditions of the English working class in a society plagued by financial turbulence. Though dwarfed by the significance of Orwell's later works, *Keep the Aspidistra Flying* has retrospectively become a renowned character study and one of his best-loved works.

SUMMARY

A STRUGGLING POET

Gordon Comstock is a bitter and impoverished 29-year-old who works in a bookshop. It is late November, and he spends his day internally insulting customers, predicting war and oncoming chaos, and lamenting his stalling career as a poet. He has convinced himself that money is the only thing stopping his success, though he is suffering a long period of writer's block. He goes home and, after dodging his landlady and fellow lodgers, attempts unsuccessfully to make progress on his poetry while waiting for a letter from his girlfriend, Rosemary, who has not contacted him in several days.

Gordon comes from what Orwell calls a middle-middle class family, without the money or titles of gentility but still riding the prestige of entrepreneurial success during the time of Gordon's grandfather. As a result, the family seems never to do anything, not even marry or bear children, and it is left to Gordon, who is the sole heir of the Comstock family, to suffer the expectation of success and to re-earn the family's fortune. He briefly describes his life, his parents' decision to put almost all the family's resources into his schooling, his hatred of modern British society's fixation on money, and his formative dislike of his family's attitudes to it. After leaving school he got a job at a PR firm as a copywriter's assistant. He found that he was exceptionally good at copywriting but hated the fact that he was a part of the money-driven world of modern marketing. As such, after a while he got his friend Ravelston, a rich literary figure, to get him a job in the bookshop so that he can focus on writing, and not money. As the years slipped by, however, he found himself more and more drained by his poverty and starved of artistic inspiration, becoming just like those few remaining members of his family, such as his sister, Julia, who stumble through a poverty-stricken life clinging on to airs of respectability.

The next day, Gordon has the afternoon off and goes to his literary critic friend Paul Doring's house for a get-together. He is dismayed when he turns up to the house to find it empty, and wanders around London in a depressed mood for the rest of the afternoon and evening, blaming his lack of money for his problems. On returning home, his night is made worse when he receives a rejection letter from a magazine that he had sent a poem to. He writes a short and brutal letter to Rosemary and goes to bed.

THE NEXT DAY

Soon after, Gordon goes to the pub with Ravelston, who is decent, a Socialist but also quite rich. Driven by this contradiction and his own financial inferiority, Gordon drunkenly rants about the contempt people have for him because of his relative poverty, and his dislike of wealthy Socialists, much to Ravelston's discomfort. Gordon further reveals that he believes women distance themselves from him because of his poverty – particularly Rosemary. He admits finally that he is still angry about having been snubbed by Paul Doring, and he returns home and writes a rude note to him.

ROSEMARY

The next day, Gordon bumps into Rosemary and the two make up. He attempts to persuade her to sleep with him, but she continually refuses. They argue about money, with him accusing her of hating him for his poverty and refusing to let her pay for his dinner. They nonetheless remain on good terms and agree to go out to the countryside together on the next Sunday. When the day comes, they have a wonderful time in the country, until a resolute Gordon insists on spending all his money on lunch. He is worried by this, and grows more worried still when Rosemary declines to sleep with him due to his refusal to spend money on contraception. They walk back miserably, and he is humiliated by having to ask her for bus-money.

Gordon suddenly receives a small sum of money, as a poem he submitted is accepted by an American publication. Rather than use it to assuage his money woes, however, he immediately calls up Ravelston and Rosemary and splurges the lot on a night out at a nice restaurant. He gets uproariously drunk, embarrassing both of his friends, and when Rosemary goes home coerces Ravelston into picking up two prostitutes. Ravelston is mortified but sticks it out to look after his friend. When they get to the hotel, however, Gordon is too drunk to do anything and passes out on the bed. He wakes up in a prison cell, having been arrested for being drunk and disorderly. He spends most of the day in the police station, until Ravelston picks him up and pays his fine.

For the next few days, Gordon lives with Ravelston, though he is desperately embarrassed and depressed at having to sponge off his friend. He finds out that due to his arrest he has lost his job, and half-heartedly visits the surrounding booksellers in search of a new one. Rosemary comes to visit him to ask him to take back his copywriting job, but he refuses, still resolutely refusing to re-enter the world of money. They argue, and Gordon finds that he is bored by her tears, sinking into apathy and self-pity. The next day he is offered a job at a bookshop's subsidiary lending library at a pitifully low wage – which he accepts because of its drudgery and lack of hope.

A CHANGE OF SCENERY

He finds a room in a dreadful, squalid lodging, and seems to be deliberately embracing the downward spiral of his life. He no longer writes poetry and instead willingly succumbs to a life of poverty and squalor. Ravelston, Rosemary and Julia all beg him to continue to hope – with Rosemary even guaranteeing him a job at his old copywriting firm – but he refuses, claiming to be trying to live outside of the money-dominated society by rejecting the power of money. In a last desperate bid to show him that she loves him and prise him from his depressive state of mind, Rosemary visits Gordon at his lodgings and sleeps with him, though neither of them seems to particularly enjoy the experience.

He continues with this lifeless existence, until one day Rosemary returns and reveals that she is pregnant. She leaves the decision-making to him, and he decides eventually to marry her and take the job at the ad agency. Though he feels that he has failed in his war over money, he is secretly relieved at being 'forced' into getting a good job and becoming comfortable and respectable. He revels in the power of fatherhood and the book ends with him and Rosemary moving into their new flat, and Gordon demanding that they should buy an aspidistra – a symbol of their newfound respectability.

CHARACTER STUDY

GORDON COMSTOCK

Gordon Comstock is described early on as "not thirty yet, but moth-eaten already" (p. 4), a thin, bedraggled and idealistic poet working as a book-seller in London. He has had one published collection – *Mice* – and is working on his follow-up, a 2000-line epic about a day out in London called *London Pleasures*. Though he is sometimes successful in his poetry submissions, he is bitterly uncertain about his artistic competence and has been stuck on his latest work for two years. He comes from a middle-middle-class English family, whose fortunes rose with a successful Victorian industrialist grandfather, and fell with subsequent generations of failure and poverty, who: "just drifted along in an atmosphere of semi-gentile failure" (p. 41). The family therefore has the pretensions of gentility, without the resources to back it up. Most of the family's money has been thrown into Gordon's education in the vain hope that he will come good and restore the family to wealth. However, as a result of this upbringing, he is obsessive about money, its power and its symbolic resonance behind every action in English society: "Money, once again; all is money. All human relationships must be purchased with money. If you have no money, men won't care for you" (p. 14). He claims to have waged war on what he calls the 'money-world' and as a result has shunned the opportunities gifted to him by his education, quitting his 'good' job as a copywriter to work for inadequate wages at a bookshop – much to his family's discontent.

Despite this anarchistic approach to Capitalist society, money still manages to dominate his life, and he complains constantly of his poverty and the way he perceives that people treat him because of it: "He took it for granted that people would snub him and forget about him. Why not, indeed? He had no money. When you have no money, your life is one long series of snubs" (p. 73). This conflict between Gordon's idealistic rejection of money and its importance in society, and his psychological insecurities about money and his lack of it drive the narrative as his friends and relatives attempt to understand and interact with him. Rosemary's frustration is summed up towards the end of the novel: the woman to whom he is eventually married reflects on "these meaningless scruples which she had never understood but which she had accepted merely because they were his. She felt all the impotence, the resentment of a woman who sees an abstract idea triumphing over common sense" (p. 217). During the final third of the novel, having lost his job after a drunken night out in London, Gordon's usual bad temper and irritability are replaced by a morbid and hopeless depression, "sinking effortless into grey, deadly failure" (p. 240). He is an educated man who in effect chooses a life of poverty on principle, only succumbing to the 'money-world' at the prospect of fatherhood. Though his actions are born from romantic idealism, his attitudes and insecurities towards money, and particularly women, cause a great deal of pain to the people around him.

RAVELSTON

Ravelston is the editor of *Antichrist*, a left-wing monthly magazine, and friend of Gordon's. He a member of the upper classes, with a large income, and is wholly embarrassed by it. This embarrassment seems to dominate his kind, generous and submissive personality: "the truth was that in every moment of his life he was apologising, tacitly, for the largeness of his income" (p. 89). Ravelston is what Orwell calls a "parlour Socialist", meaning one whose political ideals of equality and economic egalitarianism are contradicted by their upper-class lifestyle. An example of this trait can be found when he dines on steak at an upmarket restaurant with his girlfriend, all the while worrying about the unemployed in Middlesbrough. Though he and Gordon are good friends, and largely remain so throughout the novel, the difference in their incomes spawns some resentment, particularly when the obsessively proud Gordon is forced to borrow money from him.

Ravelston is representative of much of the liberal elite with whom Orwell would have had dealings in London around the time, particularly those in charge of various aspects of the publishing industry. Indeed, his portrayal of Ravelston has been said to be inspired by Orwell's good friend and editor at *The Adelphi* (a famous London literary journal) Sir Richard Rees, and *Antichrist* by many of the popular left-wing magazines of the time, which were filled with idealistic Socialist values. Orwell critiques such publications in *Keep the Aspidistra Flying*: *"Antichrist* existed to point out-that life under a decaying capitalism is deathly and meaningless. But this knowledge was only theoretical. You can't really *feel* that kind of thing when your income is eight hundred a year" (p. 92).

ROSEMARY

Rosemary and Gordon see each other romantically throughout the novel, having met at the advertising company New Albion. She is "a strong, agile girl, with stiff black hair, a small triangular face and very pronounced eyebrows" (p. 119). She is "the youngest child of one of those huge, hungry families which still exist here and there in the middle classes" (p. 123), and is unwaveringly kind and forgiving of Gordon ("whom she adored", p. 124) throughout the novel, although she is exasperated by his obstinacy and occasional cruelty. She cares deeply for Gordon and does everything she can to assuage his suffering without contaminating his ideals, but is still vilified by him for her actions. In the novel Rosemary is also described by Gordon in terms of her sexual immaturity, as she is unwilling to lose her virginity before getting married. This caution is, of course, proved to be quite reasonable, given that she falls pregnant instantly after succumbing to Gordon's desires.

ANALYSIS

HISTORICAL CONTEXT

Keep the Aspidistra Flying takes place in 1934, a uniquely turbulent point in history when much of Western Europe was both still recovering from the devastation of the First World War (1914-18) and gearing up for the Second World War (1939-45). Hitler was already in power in Germany, as was Mussolini in Italy, and speculation of war can be seen throughout the novel, as commented on by the some-times-morbid Gordon: "war is coming soon. You can't doubt it when you see the Bovex ads" (p. 257). Though war was still some way off, the period was marked by increasing global tensions, and the growing significance of dis-tinctly contrasting politics. For example, the popularity of Socialism amongst the English liberal elite can be seen in the hypocritical cha-racter of Ravelston and his left-wing magazine *Antichrist*: "you can be a Socialist *and* have a good time" (p. 109).

The period can also be defined by both a rampant commercialism in the Western world and financial disaster. Following the Wall Street Crash of 1929, the collapse of the American economy spread across the world, sparking the Great Depression. In Britain, a Conservative-led coalition government had introduced stringent welfare and budget cuts, hitting in particular the working-class industrial areas of Britain whose dependence on world trade meant mass unemployment and reliance on state benefits. In London, where the novel is set, we see a different society, dominated by glossy adverts and billboards, nice restaurants and literary magazines. The contrast between these two social factors, namely a dominant Capitalist system and crushing financial meltdown, can be seen in the horrific inequality in some of the book, and in the differing conditions of the various lodgings Gordon stays in.

A CHANGING WORLD

The novel is also an exploration of the ways in which modern English society has changed, albeit seen through the eyes of the money-obsessed Gordon. He sees the world as one that is completely dominated by money, to the point that "Money-worship has been elevated into a religion [...] Money is what God used to be" (p. 46). Indeed, the novel follows his attempts to escape this sort of world by denouncing the power of money, though as we see, the misery of his money-less life shows clearly that he fails in this endeavour. The world of *Keep the Aspidistra Flying* is a superficial one in which money decides everything about a person's life: "Money again, always money! Lack of money means discomfort, means squalid worries, means shortage of tobacco, means ever-present consciousness of failure – above all, it means loneliness" (p. 33). Gordon's lack of money prevents him from marrying, from writing great poetry and from cultivating an acceptable social life. Though much of this comes as part of a satire of Gordon's almost caricatural obsession with money, the social power of wealth is clear to see both in the novel and in society in general, particularly in those like the kind and wealthy Ravelston: "Money and culture! In a country like England you can no more be cultured without money than you can join the Cavalry Club!" (p. 8).

Huge burgeoning advertising industries are also depicted in the novel, and the many billboards and posters advertising various brands and products represent to Gordon this very money-obsessed world. It is for this reason that he gives up his job as a copywriter, so as not to perpetuate the money-worship he sees around him. He explains his revelation on finding himself to be good at the work: "*This* then, was what he was coming to! Writing lies to tickle the money out of fools' pockets!" (p. 58). Beyond Gordon's despair can be seen Orwell's own critique of what he perceives to be a rapidly deteriorating world:

> "For can you not see [...] that behind that slick self-satisfaction, that tittering fat-bellied triviality, there is nothing but a frightful emptiness, a secret despair? The great death-wish of the modern world. Suicide pacts. Heads stuck in gas-ovens in lonely maisonettes. French letters and Amen pills. The reverberations of future wars. Enemy aeroplanes flying over London..." (p. 16).

As such, for both Gordon and Orwell, poetry is an escape from this sort of world, a pursuit made romantic largely by the fact of its financial unviability.

THE ENGLISH CLASS SYSTEM

A novel so dominated by the theme of money in English society is of course concerned with the English class system and its effects on the people within it. Orwell is well known in his work for continually defining characters by their place in the English class system and, indeed, we get just a few lines into the descriptions of certain people before we get a detailed analysis of how exactly their characters have been shaped by their family's place in the English class system. Gordon's family, for example, are described as part of the middle-middle class, a money-less, landless and title-less pseudo-gentry. He says of them:

"It was not merely a lack of money. It was rather that, having no money, they still lived mentally in the money-world – the world in which money is virtue and poverty is crime. It was not poverty but the down-dragging of respectable poverty that had done for them. They had accepted the money code and by that code they were failures" (p. 47).

It is clear that this sort of upbringing has shaped Gordon's outlook on life, as a person who both despises money for its social importance, and yet desires it for the same reason. It can be said of such characters in Orwell's work that the exaggerated nature of their class characteristics makes them caricatural representations of class. Gordon attempts to break away from the sense of respectability held at the heart of the English middle classes by deliberately living in squalor and disrepute, but succumbs in the end to returning to his decent job and flying high the symbol of the aspidistra.

THE ASPIDISTRA AS A SYMBOL

The aspidistra was a popular plant in middle-class Victorian society, renowned for thriving in a variety of environments. As such, to Gordon in *Keep the Aspidistra Flying*, the plant is a powerful symbol of the kind of middle-class respectability and pretension that he is desperate to avoid, and it haunts him everywhere he goes:

> "The aspidistra became sort of a symbol for Gordon after that. The aspidistra, flower of England! It ought to be on our coat of arms instead of the lion and the unicorn. There will be no revolution in England while there are aspidistras in the windows" (p. 47).

To accept the aspidistra is to accept the power and importance of the financial stability, pride in reputation and professional dependency of English middle-class life. The novel explores Gordon's relationship with this symbol and his eventual yielding to a more conventional, financially viable life associated with a man of his class and education. This is represented by his vehement buying of an aspidistra when he moves in with Rosemary at the end of the novel. Indeed, his attitudes to the aspidistra and its symbolic meaning change when he finds out that he is to become a father, seeing the importance and necessity of the sort of regularity that the plant represents when raising a family:

> "They kept themselves respectable – kept the aspidistra flying. Besides they were alive. They were bound up in the bundle of life. They begot children, which is what the saints and the soul savers never by any chance do. The aspidistra is the tree of life, he thought suddenly" (p. 268).

FURTHER REFLECTION

SOME QUESTIONS TO THINK ABOUT...

- What signs can be seen in the novel of the coming war? Is Gordon correct in his speculation?
- Gordon's idealism could be perceived as noble, in its rejection of the power of money. Should he be seen as a heroic character despite the way he treats the people close to him?
- Gordon lives in a world that he believes is dominated by money. To what extent is this view of the world distorted by his personality? Is what he sees the truth?
- Consider the role of women in the book. How is Rosemary treated unfairly because of her gender?
- Are Orwell's criticisms of Ravelston valid? Can a person be a Socialist and yet still enjoy the fruits of their wealth?
- Can we see the development of Orwell's subsequent books in *Keep the Aspidistra Flying*? What ideas relating to *1984* and *Animal Farm* can be found in the novel?

- In what ways is British national identity presented in the book?
- Discuss the importance of the English class system in defining the novel's characters. Is Gordon solely a product of his class?

We want to hear from you!
Leave a comment on your online library
and share your favourite books on social media!

FURTHER READING

REFERENCE EDITION

- Orwell, G. (1998) *Keep the Aspidistra Flying*. London: Martin Secker & Warburg Limited.

REFERENCE STUDIES

- Orwell, G. (2000) *Homage to Catalonia*. London: Penguin Books Ltd.

ADDITIONAL SOURCES

- Taylor, D. J. (2003) *Orwell: The Life*. London: Chatto & Windus.

MORE FROM BRIGHTSUMMARIES.COM

- Reading guide – *1984* by George Orwell.

- Reading guide – *Animal Farm* by George Orwell.

- Reading guide – *Burmese Days* by George Orwell.

- Reading guide – *Coming Up for Air* by George Orwell.

- Reading guide – *Down and Out in Paris and London* by George Orwell.

- Reading guide – *Homage to Catalonia* by George Orwell.

- Reading guide – *The Road to Wigan Pier* by George Orwell.

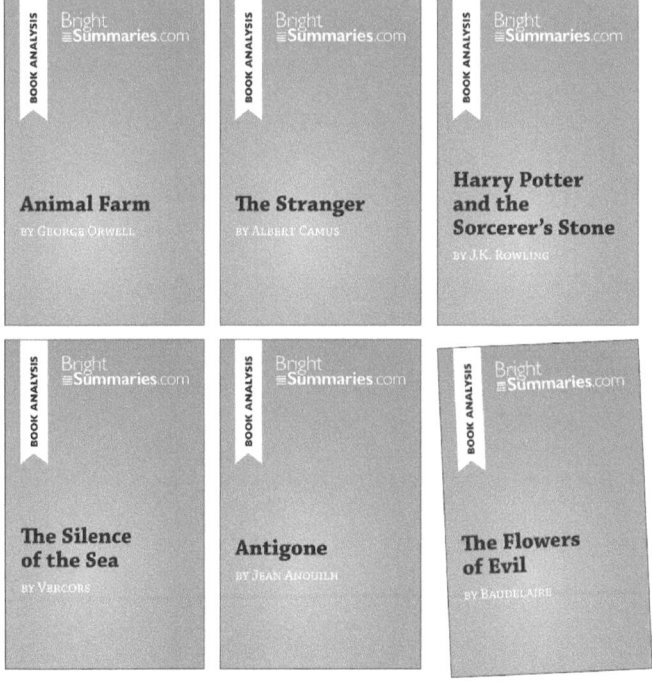

www.brightsummaries.com

Ebook EAN: 9782808015738

Paperback EAN: 9782808015745

Legal Deposit: D/2018/12603/545

Cover: © Primento

Digital conception by Primento, the digital partner of
publishers.